Teens and Rural Sports
Rodeos, Horses, Hunting, and Fishing

Title List

Getting Ready for the Fair: Crafts, Projects, and Prize-Winning Animals

Growing Up on a Farm: Responsibilities and Issues

Migrant Youth: Falling Between the Cracks

Rural Crime and Poverty: Violence, Drugs, and Other Issues

Rural Teens and Animal Raising: Large and Small Pets

Rural Teens and Nature: Conservation and Wildlife Rehabilitation

Rural Teens on the Move:
Cars, Motorcycles, and Off-Road Vehicles

Teen Life Among the Amish and Other Alternative Communities:
Choosing a Lifestyle

Teen Life on Reservations and in First Nation Communities:
Growing Up Native

Teen Minorities in Rural North America: Growing Up Different

Teens and Rural Education: Opportunities and Challenges

Teens and Rural Sports: Rodeos, Horses, Hunting, and Fishing

Teens Who Make a Difference in Rural Communities:
Youth Outreach Organizations and Community Action

Teens and Rural Sports
Rodeos, Horses, Hunting, and Fishing

by Roger Smith

Mason Crest Publishers

Philadelphia

Mason Crest Publishers Inc.
370 Reed Road
Broomall, Pennsylvania 19008
(866) MCP-BOOK (toll free)
www.masoncrest.com

First printing
1 2 3 4 5 6 7 8 9 10
ISBN 978-1-4222-0011-7 (series)

Library of Congress Cataloging-in-Publication Data

Smith, Roger, 1959 Aug. 15–
  Teens and rural sports : rodeos, horses, hunting, and fishing / by Roger Smith.
      p. cm. — (Youth in rural North America)
  Includes bibliographical references and index.
  ISBN-13: 978-1-4222-0022-3
  1. Outdoor recreation—United States—Juvenile literature. 2. Outdoor life—United States—Juvenile literature. 3. Rural youth—United States—Juvenile literature. 4. Sports—United States—Juvenile literature. I. Title.
GV191.4S65 2008
796.0835—dc22
                                          2006033186

Cover and interior design by MK Bassett-Harvey.
Produced by Harding House Publishing Service, Inc.
www.hardinghousepages.com

Cover image design by Peter Spires Culotta.
Cover photography by iStock Photography (Robyn Glover,
    Nathan McClunie, and Jim Lopes).
Printed in Malaysia by Phoenix Press.

Contents

Introduction

by Celeste Carmichael

Results of a survey published by the Kellogg Foundation reveal that most people consider growing up in the country to be idyllic. And it's true that growing up in a rural environment does have real benefits. Research indicates that families in rural areas consistently have more traditional values, and communities are more closely knit. Rural youth spend more time than their urban counterparts in contact with agriculture and nature. Often youth are responsible for gardens and farm animals, and they benefit from both their sense of responsibility and their understanding of the natural world. Studies also indicate that rural youth are more engaged in their communities, working to improve society and local issues. And let us not forget the psychological and aesthetic benefits of living in a serene rural environment!

The advantages of rural living cannot be overlooked—but neither can the challenges. Statistics from around the country show that children in a rural environment face many of the same difficulties that are typically associated with children living in cities, and they fare worse than urban kids on several key indicators of positive youth development. For example, rural youth are more likely than their urban counterparts to use drugs and alcohol. Many of the problems facing rural youth are exacerbated by isolation, lack of jobs (for both parents and teens), and lack of support services for families in rural communities.

When most people hear the word "rural," they instantly think "farms." Actually, however, less than 12 percent of the population in rural areas make their livings through agriculture. Instead, service jobs are the top industry in rural North America. The lack of opportunities for higher paying jobs can trigger many problems: persistent poverty, lower educational standards, limited access to health care, inadequate housing, underemployment of teens, and lack of extracurricular possibilities. Additionally, the lack of—or in some cases surge of—diverse populations in rural communities presents its own set of challenges for youth and communities. All these concerns lead to the greatest threat to rural communities: the mass exodus of the post–high school population. Teens relocate for educational, recreational, and job opportunities, leaving their hometown indefinitely deficient in youth capital.

This series of books offers an in-depth examination of both the pleasures and challenges for rural youth. Understanding the realities is the first step to expanding the options for rural youth and increasing the likelihood of positive youth development.

CHAPTER 1
Rodeo

It is a warm Fourth of July night in Kayenta, Arizona. Not far away, the awe-inspiring mesas of Monument Valley stand silently in the moonlight, but no one is thinking of those now. Tonight is the final evening of the Multi-Sanctioned Kayenta Rodeo, and the stands are full of fans—mostly Navajo, all wearing broad-brimmed hats, jeans, and boots.

Rodeo competitions are fun—and dangerous!

Events come one after another in quick succession: roping, bare-back riding, and now barrel racing. The announcer introduces Kassidy Dennison, and the crowd cheers. Kassidy and her horse come out of the gate like a shot, dance around the barrels in liquid motion, then jet back toward the gate as the audience stomps and cheers. It is an amazing combination of grace and raw speed—blink and you miss her. Later in the evening, after the crowd has watched the death-defying bull-riding event and a spectacular fireworks display, Kassidy walks into the center of the arena to claim her prize for the rodeo: a brand new horse trailer and more than a thousand dollars—not bad for a thirteen-year-old seventh-grader! Furthermore, this evening is just one in a string of successes culminating in her

Youth in the rural West take pride in their rodeo skills.

winning the Indian National Finals Rodeo women's all-around championship title for 2005.

A *Navajo Times* article lends insight into the life of this outstanding young cowgirl. Every single day, whether it is hot or cold, dry or snowing, Kassidy helps her family care for their sixteen horses at her home in Tohatchi, New Mexico. She claims that she learned to ride before she learned to walk. Rodeo is a true family sport for the Dennisons; in 2005, Kassidy's brother Kyle competed in steer-wrestling and calf-roping events, and her sister Devyn competed in breakaway roping.

In the *Navajo Times* article, Kassidy shares her tips on succeeding in rodeo: "Just do your best, practice every day. Rodeo can be difficult," she says. "But keep trying to get it right. It's not something to goof around about, it's too expensive to play around with." When asked to name her role models, Kassidy said, "My whole family." Her mother also believes in rodeo as a family event: "It's a family sport. It doesn't work when you're not in it together. You have to have your family," she said. "We're a family who believes in [rodeo] and supports it."

Rural Sports and Rodeo

Teen life in rural areas can be difficult in some ways. Rural families tend to not to make as much money as those in suburban areas; isolation from urban centers means less options educationally, **vocationally**, and socially, and greater distance from medical facilities. However, life away from cities can offer substantial rewards as well. Rural teens can more easily participate in outdoor sports such as rodeo, horseback riding, hunting, and fishing. While rural teens participate in many of the same team sports as their city-dwelling **peers**, the availability of open spaces such as nearby fields and woods enable them to do things that urban kids rarely get to do.

Many Native young adults excel at rodeo events.

Participation in outdoor recreation in turn helps rural teens develop value systems somewhat different from urban kids. Rural teens are more likely to connect with animals: they develop close relationships with dogs and horses, which serve as four-footed companions. At the same time, however, they know that animals provide food, both in the form of domesticated herd animals and wild game. Rodeo illustrates the ways people and animals form mutually beneficial relationships: horse and rider must act as one to compete effectively in any rodeo event.

Rodeo is more than a sport; it is a centuries old tradition in the Americas. Mexican *vaqueros* and North American cowboys competed, informally at first, with the skills they used for their livelihood: roping cattle, wrestling cows to the ground, riding unbroken broncos. They also indulged in feats of sheer bravado, racing their horses and even riding enormous, vicious bulls. These events were eventually formalized as today's sport.

Today, rodeo is more popular than ever before, with more than 13 million viewers tuning into the rodeo finals on ESPN. Typical rodeo events include bull riding, bareback bronc riding, saddle bronc riding, steer wrestling, team roping, calf roping, and women's barrel racing. Rodeo is more than a sport, for those who live in it. As one teen bull rider put it, "My family supports me in every way they can and so does almost everyone else. The people that ride and rope are my extended family and, honestly, I don't think I could live without them."

Bull Riding: The Most Dangerous Rodeo Event

All rodeo events require skill and practice, but bull riding is by far the most dangerous. Rodeo bulls are far from friendly creatures; a typical adult weighs 2,000 pounds (907 kilograms), and bulls hate

Why Do It?

Statistically, the chances of getting killed bull riding are relatively slim: in an average year, 3 of 100,000 rodeo contestants die from sport-related injuries. That being said, it is still obviously dangerous. A 2,000-pound animal with sharp horns and nasty disposition is always a threat. Whether the rider is thrown or dismounts, he or she still is in danger while in the ring with the bull. World Champion Lane Frost, one of the greatest bull riders in history, died in 1989 when a bull gored him after he dismounted. So why do bull riders do it? One teen bull rider explains on his personal Web site:

> People ask why we would do something like this and take the chance of getting hurt or even worse. Most Bull Riders would say that they do it because it's an adrenalin rush. Others would say it's for the money. This year the PBR is putting up $1,000,000 for the winner on top of the year end winnings. Some of them are doing it just to help keep the sport of rodeo alive to themselves and the rest of the world.

A sign in rural Arizona advertises an upcoming rodeo event.

having people try to ride them. When a bull rider comes flying out the gate of the bullpen, he is in for the wildest eight seconds of his life. In an age of extreme sports, bull riding may still be the most extreme sport in the world.

For thirteen-year-old Preston of Kayenta Arizona, almost everything in life revolves around horses, cattle, and the rodeo. He's been injured by a bull—the beast hit him in the head, resulting in eight stitches above Preston's left eye—but he was back riding bulls in a week. His favorite movie is *8 Seconds*, the dramatized account of Lane Frost's life riding bulls, and Preston's life goal is to be a world champion in rodeo. He wants rodeo to be his career, and he wants to be the best. He'd like to compete on horseback, too, riding bareback, saddling bronc, team roping, and ribbon roping. Like many other young Navajo rodeo riders, Preston inherited his interest in the sport from his ancestors; he says his family have been "into rodeo" for many generations.

Rodeo Helps Ensure the Future of Rural Lifestyles

According to a November 2005 article originally published in the *Edmonton Journal*, Canadian farmers and ranchers are struggling with challenges posed by high fuel prices, fear of **Mad Cow Disease**, and other factors. Though some troubled country dwellers are tempted to sell their rural businesses and move to the city, according to the article, their children help them to stay put and hope for a better future. Nine-year-old Dakota says, "Mom and Dad, sometimes they want to move to the city, but I talk them out of it." Dakota loves to ride horses and dreams of taking over the family farm some day. Reporter Tim Lai spoke with a number of children and teens at the 2005 Canadian Rodeo Finals and heard a number of similar sentiments: participation in rodeo and other cultural events helps tomorrow's farmers and ranchers keep an optimistic attitude toward their future.

CHAPTER 2

Horses

Seventeen-year-old Erin inherited a love for horses from her grandmother, who always hoped her grandchildren would love horses as she did. Erin's grandmother provided riding lessons for Erin when she was only ten. Little did Erin know that at the age of sixteen, she would be around horses all the time.

Her family moved outside of Payson, a little town in northern Arizona. They live at an altitude of 6,000 feet (1828.8 meters), in the middle of a ponderosa pine forest at Tonto Rim Christian Camp. She is part of a four-person team of wranglers in charge of the horses at the camp and she loves it; her grandmother's wish has come true.

For thousands of years, young men and women have enjoyed riding horses. Teens who own horses in Canada and the United States are continuing an age-old heritage: cowboys, cowgirls, vaqueros, and other *equestrians* helped settle North America. Teens who love riding and caring for their horses today carry on this honored tradition of horsemanship.

Daily Routines and Trail Rides

When campers are at Tonto Rim, Erin works all day taking care of the horses. She feeds the horses at seven o'clock in the morning, and the four wranglers *muck* the stalls while the horses have their individually prepared breakfasts. All the horses get alfalfa hay, but individuals get different amounts of hard feed according to their specific needs. When the feeding and chores are finished, the campers can then enjoy riding the horses.

Erin helps groom and saddle the herd for trail rides. The wranglers know which horses work together well and which ones need to stay apart. Within a herd or group of horses there are different personalities: some horses are shy, some are bossy, some are friends, and some are enemies—relationships within the herd help them bond. In the Tonto Rim herd, Charley is the lead horse because he is the most aggressive stallion—the top male. The lineup continues with friends placed beside friends, passers placed toward the front, and horses that don't mind trailing behind at the rear. Erin says they're like little kids with their own personalities, likes, and dislikes.

Eight to ten campers go on a trail ride at a time. Once they are securely in their saddles, Erin gives them the rules and the trail ride begins. Trail rides last from fifteen to sixty minutes, depending on the age of the campers. However, some camps are devoted totally to horsemanship activities and can have trail rides lasting up to eight

A Native American girl enjoys spending time with her family's horse.

No one knows who was the first human being to ride on a horse—but today, countless young adults growing up in the country find happiness on the back of a horse!

No one knows for sure who first rode on a horse's back. Scientists believe the first equestrians mastered riding approximately 6,000 years ago on the grassy plains of eastern Europe. The horses they rode would have been smaller than our horses, with stiff upstanding manes like zebras. The first horseback ride was an event in history as important as the invention of the sailing ship or the bow and arrow. A horse and rider had advantages over either a horse or human by themselves. Spanish explorers brought the horse to North America, and they quickly became popular with First Nation peoples and Native Americans.

hours. At most of the camps on Tonto Rim, there are usually three or four trail rides each day. Between rides, the horses are tied up in trail order in an arena, and campers can enjoy visiting with them, up close and personal.

When the last trail riders have returned to the camp, the wranglers unsaddle the horses and groom them. They inspect each animal for any medical needs. Ointment is applied to any saddle sores or cuts. If the hair under the saddle looks a little clumpy, the horse may have some bacteria on its back; a little spray of Listerine mouthwash takes care of the problem. Finally, the wranglers lead the horses back into their stalls, keeping them in the same order as they were on trail rides to make sure things are peaceful in the horse barn.

Erin helps operate several camps focused on horsemanship; these include junior, senior, and adult horsemanship camps. During these sessions, riders are taught how to care for the horses and how to handle them in gallop and jumping situations.

Tonto Rim has a variety of horse breeds—Appaloosa, Arabians, and quarter horses. Normally these breeds might be too full of life for ordinary trail rides, but the camp buys these horses when they are older and less active. Erin has bonded with one horse in particular—Zach, a chestnut quarter horse. She loves his personality, and he seems to be especially fond of her, too; sometimes he refuses to let other wranglers put a *bit* in his mouth.

Horse Clubs and Camps

Horses are expensive pets to buy and maintain. Because they cost thousands of dollars a year for food, medical care, supplies, and emergencies, not all rural youth can afford to keep a horse. They can be difficult to care for, needing daily attention for feeding, exercising, and grooming.

Camps provide a way for horse lovers to experience the pleasures of horseback riding, without the expense of owning one. Horse camps can be found all over the United States and Canada. Most of them last a week and provide many horsemanship-related experiences. Campers may learn how to feed a horse, how to handle and groom them, and how to recognize common ailments. They may also learn how to handle the tack, or the saddlery, which is the equipment the horse or pony wears when ridden.

Rural horse lovers may also join 4-H horse clubs. At the turn of the nineteenth century, educators felt the need to improve life in rural areas and they began 4-H clubs to address those needs. Improved methods of farming and homemaking were the main emphasis in the beginning years. In 1907, the U.S. Department of Agriculture began 4-H programs under the Cooperative Extension

Despite their size, horses can be gentle pets.

Service. Under the leadership of Seaman Knapp, the father of the Cooperative Extension Service, these clubs evolved into today's 4-H clubs. Gertrude Warren was the first to begin calling the organizations "4-H clubs"; she is often referred to as the "mother" of the 4-H clubs. Oscar H. Benson, one of the early founders of 4-H, is credited with the idea of using the four-leaf clover as the club emblem. Originally, the four Hs represented, head, heart, hand, and hustle. Benson wrote, "A leader with *head* trained to think, plan, reason; with *heart* trained to be true, kind, and sympathetic; and with *hands* trained to be useful, helpful, and skillful; and the *hustle* to render ready service, to develop health and vitality." The hustle was later changed to "health." By 1915, there were 4-H programs in forty-seven states.

Canadians also began forming clubs for youth in the early 1900s. The Provincial Ministries of Agriculture began these clubs to improve agriculture, increase production, and enrich rural life. They called these clubs "boys and girls clubs." In 1952, they adopted the name of 4-H club, but they do not affiliate with the U.S. club. According to the Canadian 4-H Web site, there are more than 33,000 4-H members age nine to twenty-one and 10,500 volunteer leaders in 2,500 clubs across Canada.

The Foothills Lighthorse 4-H club of Gull Lake, Saskatchewan, meets once a month so members can practice riding when the weather is warm. During the cold winter months, members do projects such as tack boxes and bridles, saddle strands, and belts. Once a year they participate in an achievement day, when they hold competitions in riding, judging, record books, and questionnaires. They also have public-speaking contests, with the winners competing against other club members. The winners of those contests go on to compete at the provincial level.

Among many goals and aims for their members, the Foothills Lighthorse 4-H club emphasizes horse-handling skills, knowledge of horse safety precautions, and horse nutrition, such as how to feed a horse a balanced diet. They learn how to identify horse diseases and

4-H club members often bring their horses to the fair to show them in competition with other horses. This horse at the county fair in Tioga County, New York, gets a visit from a young passerby.

Jumping is one of the many horsemanship skills a young person might learn in a 4-H club.

The 4-H Pledge

I pledge: My head to clearer thinking My heart to greater loyalty My hands to larger service and My health to better living for my club, my community, my country, and my world.

parasites and how to recognize unsoundness of the horse. Members develop responsibility and pride in owning their horses. Just like U.S. 4-H clubs, the motto of Canadian clubs is, "Learn by doing": they expect that members will own a horse.

Horse club activities sponsored by 4-H in the United States vary from club to club. Many clubs teach grooming, horsemanship, horse and tack care, and riding techniques. Some sponsor horse clinics, horse drill teams, and demonstration horse show competitions. Some horse clubs include horse lovers who don't own their own horses, but still want to learn about them.

In many states, 4-H clubs sponsor a yearly Horse Bowl and *hippology* contest. These contests do not involve the physical presence of horses, but give an opportunity for 4-H members to show how much they have learned about the various horse topics. For the Horse Bowl, youth learn scientific information about *genetics*, reproduction, herd health and behavior, nutrition, and reproduction. In the hippology contest, youth demonstrate skills learned about horse judging, identification of tack and equipment, horse-related products, and scientific information.

Taking care of a horse teaches teens responsibility as it provides them with satisfaction and increased self-confidence.

Yearly 4-H horse club competitions are held at the University of Illinois campus at Champaign-Urbana. Along with the Horse Bowl and hippology contest, there is also a horse demonstration/illustration talk contest, and a public-speaking contest. Educators not only help 4-H teens learn about horses and horse topics in their club, but through these contests, they help teens gain the skills in demonstrating or illustrating what they have learned. They also work to develop the ability to speak in public and to inform others about horse related subjects and the 4-H program. The goals of 4-H educators are to help members develop courage, persuasiveness, and self-confidence.

Not all rural teens can own or have access to a real horse, but teens living in the small town of Salmon, Idaho, can join a 4-H-model horse club. There members learn about breeds, colors, and markings of various horses. They learn to make model-size saddles, bridles, and halters. They go on to participate in model horse shows, where their horses are judged in the same way as regular horse shows. Participants have to know the rules and pay close attention to details. The judges will disqualify a horse if the halter is too loose or the saddle pad crooked. With this experience, should the teens someday have a horse, they will be well-versed in the ins-and-outs of horse competitions.

A Horse Lover in Alberta

Tiffani is a member of a 4-H club in Perryvale, Alberta, Canada. The club meets several times a month and is only thirty minutes away from her home. Tiffani loves living in the country where it is quiet, away from the noise of city traffic. Well, it is not always quiet—she can hear coyotes calling at night, and sometimes in the spring the family can hear baby moose and deer calling to their mothers. The neighing of horses is also a common sound on their property. Her

Many rural children begin riding horses when they are still quite small.

The Tennessee Walking Horse is known for its kindly disposition, gentle manner, and its desire to please. It is one of the most versatile horses. The Tennessee Walking Horse Youth Association Web site claims that these horses are great for successfully competing in such disciplines as showmanship at halter, barrel racing, jumping, basic reigning and dressage, English pleasure, good seat and hands, pleasure driving, pole bending, Western pleasure, and trail obstacles.

family owns a Tennessee Walking Horse Farm that started when Tiffani was seven and wanted her own horse.

Tiffani started riding horses from the time she was a baby, because her mom liked to take her on rides. At age five, she took riding lessons, and her aunt Lana would plan trail rides with her. On one of these rides, her aunt's horse kicked at Tiffani's horse, and Tiffani's horse took off running across a newly mowed field. Tiffani couldn't stay on and flew off the horse, landing in the prickly cut hay. Her face showed the evidence with little pockmarks for some time.

During riding lessons, Tiffani continued to have a hard time staying on her horse when it ran, so her mother did some research and found that Tennessee Walking Horses or Morgans had a nice even *gait* and might be easier for Tiffani to ride. When Tiffani walked into the pen with Blazin' Socks, a registered Tennessee Walking Horse, the horse immediately came up to her and nuzzled her long blonde hair. It was love at first sight for both of them. The family didn't even go on to check out the other horse. Blaze, as they called her, was the beginning of a wonderful thing for the family. They now own ten Tennessee Walkers—or, as the family says, the horses own them.

One of Tiffani's favorite things to do was to call her best friend, Galaxy, and make plans to meet halfway between their houses. Each girl would travel two and a half miles and then meet at a creek. Tiffani had to be careful or Blaze would jump the creek. The girls would let their horses graze while they passed the time chatting. Unfortunately, Galaxy moved away, but the friends do get to spend time together at horse shows. Most of the shows and exhibits the family attends are associated with TWHBEA, the Tennessee Walking Horse Breeders and Exhibitors Association.

Daily Routines and Special Trips

Tiffani gets up every school morning at 6:30. She is responsible for getting her brother, Robert-Paul, up and ready for school. Both children have to catch the bus by 7:10. They get home from school around 4:00, and, after homework is done, Tiffani checks on her horses. She and her mom walk to the backfield and make sure the herd is doing well. Sometimes, Tiffany will ride her horse. She now has two horses, F88's Skylark, and a foal named Little Sweet Pea.

One of Tiffani's favorite family events is going on a long trail-ride weekend. They load up their horses and take them to a trailhead. When they go to Horse Creek Ranch, they ride through woods, down hillsides, and through creeks. They spend the night at the ranch and leave for home the next morning. On one of these trips, they spotted a small black bear. Another of their favorite trips is to a friend's cabin. It's only a five-mile (8.05-kilometer) ride, but they have to go on a trail through woods and very steep hills. When riding down one of these hills, they have to be careful to lean back in

Horse Grooming

The most important reason for grooming a horse is to keep its coat and skin clean and healthy. It also makes the horse look more beautiful. Most horses and ponies love to be groomed. It is a good chance for an owner to check for injuries and to assess the horse's general condition. To groom a horse after it has been in a field or on a trail, an owner should do the following:

1. Use a hoof pick to clear out mud and stones from the feet.

2. Sponge the nose, eyes, and dock with separate sponges.

3. Take off mud with a rubber curry comb.

4. Brush using a back-and-forth motion with a dandy brush over the areas where the tack goes.

Every few days brush over the entire body with a body brush and untangle the mane and tail with fingers and then brush them with the body brush.

the saddle; if they don't, it feels as though they'll flip right over the horse's head!

Tiffani loves spending time with her horses, playing with them, caring for them, riding them, and showing them. Her wish is that everyone who owns a horse would be sure to spend plenty of time with it, as people and horses can share a special relationship.

Horses Save Gas

With the rising prices of gasoline, two creative teens living in the small town of Rush Valley, Utah, forty-five miles (72.4 kilometers) south of Salt Lake City, decided to quit driving to school. The roundtrip from home to school was thirty miles (42.3 kilometers), and their car only got ten miles (16.1 kilometers) per gallon. They came up with the bright idea to ride their horses to school. Their horses, Nighthawk and Wink, spent the school day in a stall inside the school's animal laboratory. Although it took hours for the girls to get to school, they felt it was worth it, since hay was cheaper than gas. Unfortunately, the school made them stop, saying that horses on the school grounds were not allowed.

Horse Accidents

Safety is an important factor when riding a horse. According to the National Safe Kids Campaign (NSKC) Rural Injury Fact Sheet, in 2002, more than 13,400 youth fourteen years and younger were treated in emergency rooms for horse-related injuries. Head injuries are the most common cause of death and serious injuries in horse-related accidents. Approximately 40 percent of equestrian-related injuries require hospitalization.

Injuries can occur from falling off a horse, getting kicked by the horse, and being assaulted by the horse. Horses can weigh as much

Horses are not only fun and friendly pets—they also help save gasoline.

Never attempt something on horseback if you aren't certain you and your horse have the skills you need. Falls can be dangerous to both rider and animal.

> Remember:
>
> Horses can't see what is directly in front of them. If you approach from the side, the horse is less likely to become spooked.

as 1,000 pounds, and they need to be treated with respect. These animals tend to be easily excited and frightened by unexpected circumstances. Rural youth with horses learn early on to approach them in the correct manner and treat them properly.

One rural girl who shows Appaloosa horses tells of her first riding accident. While her father worked in the barn one day, she decided to take a ride in their field. She saddled up and trotted out but soon realized that she had left her helmet in the barn. She returned to the barn, put on her helmet, and went back into the field. Suddenly, and quite unexpectedly, a little brown animal popped up in front of her horse. The horse, which is usually extremely gentle and calm, became agitated and started galloping with a sharp turn to the left. The rider was not prepared and fell off, landing headfirst on a rock. Her dad was concerned when the horse returned to the barn without his daughter. He ran out and found her unharmed, but with a very dented and scratched helmet in her hand.

She advises all riders to always wear a helmet.

Another young girl was helping her family check out a horse they were thinking of buying. As she was trotting with the horse in the arena, the horse suddenly tripped, falling on its side, causing the rider's head to slam onto the ground. She was rushed to the hospital where she remained in a coma for some time. Her skull had been

The bond between a horse and a human being is one of the greatest rewards of owning this animal.

cracked across the back, and her brain had become swollen, leaving open the possibility of brain damage—if she survived. At first, the doctors were skeptical of her chances, but after two weeks, she began to recover.

Wearing a helmet can save a person's life. Even well-trained, gentle horses can become spooked and bolt unexpectedly. They can trip and fall with even the most experienced rider. Many experts in horsemanship strongly recommend that riders wear headgear.

Because the horse is such a social animal, humans and horses tend to *bond* to each other. Horses show a special devotion to their owners. For centuries, poets and storytellers have described horses as animals with a wonderful spirit, charm, and nobility, and these qualities make horses special companions. Not many animals have been the subject of so much art or poetry. Rural teens who own horses are lucky people.

CHAPTER 3

Hunting

Eighteen-year-old sportsman Matt knew what his greatest desire was before dying of Hodgkin's disease, but for the Make-a-Wish Foundation, it was a wish too controversial to grant: Matt's desire before the illness took his life was to travel to Canada and hunt a moose. The Make-A-Wish Foundation, founded in 1980, has granted 66,000 wishes to children with a life-threatening illness; the group's motto is "Our wishes are only limited to the child's imagination." However, when Matt's mother called the foundation from her home in Erie, Pennsylvania, they refused Matt's wish due to complaints the organization had received from animal rights groups when a similar request had been granted.

Matt's mother was angry, but she persisted in finding a way for her son to get his wish; she contacted sporting organizations telling them of her son's wish. In response, the dying boy's family received an amazing outpouring of generosity from the sixty-eight-resident town of Nordegg, in Alberta, Canada. An outfitter whose wife had lost an arm to cancer provided the hunt for free, and a resort lodge donated a place for Matt and his father to stay while on the trip. Other groups helped as well: a helicopter company flew them to the remote town; another company provided for Matt's license; a grocery store donated food; and a nurse took a week of vacation to travel with them in case of emergency.

Matt got his wish. He sighted and killed one huge moose with a fifty-five-inch- (139.7-centimeter-)wide *rack*. Physically drained but emotionally elated, the young man returned home to Pennsylvania and died not long after. His mother says that the anticipation of his moose hunt kept Matt going through many months of pain. "He kept saying, 'I'll be all right because I'm going on that moose hunt.'"

Is Hunting in Our Genes?

A young man sits in a treetop *blind* in a northeastern wood. The trees are mostly bare, and the ground is hidden under a blanket of brown, orange, and crimson leaves. The air is cold, still, and slightly damp; his feeling of contentment comes just from breathing pure air at the beginning of winter in a silent forest. He hears a crackle and turns to face the slight sound—a deer moving slowly through the forest beneath him! Slowly, the camouflaged youth begins to pull the arrow back on the string of his compound bow, but then pauses. The deer has a fine rack of horns, and he has only purchased an antlerless permit. The young hunter smiles to himself and relaxes his grip on the string. He still has all day to wait, and even if he doesn't get a deer, being in the woods on such a lovely, peaceful day is worth it all.

Hunters, including teen hunters, are required to display their hunting licenses on their backs.

A portable blind offers cover for two young hunters, camouflaging them while they wait for a passing deer.

Nonhunters seem genuinely puzzled by the allure of outdoor sports: "What," they ask, "is the fun in freezing out in the woods, all alone, waiting to shoot some poor animal? And why go to all the hassle of gutting and skinning and dragging the carcass (yuck!) when you can buy packaged meat in a store?" Some scientists answer that the pleasure of hunting may literally be in our very blood.

Dr. Randal Eaton of the University of Alberta says,

Both males and females may benefit much from hunting and fishing (fishing is hunting with a hook), but boys especially gain from hunting. . . . Just as females are biologically adapted to reproduce, males are adapted to hunt, kill and provide. . . . Hunting invokes an

Why He Hunts

Lance, age fifteen, from Somerset Texas, explains on Channelone.com Student Exchange why he hunts:

Hunting—whether you're for it or against it, chances are you have a very set opinion about it, but do you have all the facts? I'm an avid hunter. . . . Some people say that hunting threatens an animal population. At least with deer, the opposite is true. Without hunting, the deer population in this country would build up so much that there would not be enough food to support all of them. Many would starve during long winter months. . . . According to some, hunters don't care about the environment or conservation. This is also not true. Hunting license fees give state wildlife departments more than $185 million a year. Another $86 million each year comes from a special tax on ammunition and goes directly to the states to be spent on conservation. . . . Some people say a deer has no chance against a hunter with a high-powered rifle. This is easily disproved. According to Texas Parks and Wildlife, it takes an average hunter more than a year to take their first animal. More often than not the animal gets away.

altered state of consciousness, one of supreme alertness to the animal and the environment. It gets us out of ourselves, beyond our ego, and as a consequence the hunt is fundamentally a religious experience, one that reconnects us to the source.

Dr. Eaton notes the positive effect that a hunting experience may produce in troubled teens. There is a wilderness survival course for delinquent boys in Idaho, where they must survive with nothing more than a sleeping bag and a pocketknife. They carefully observe and study wild animals and devise weapons and traps in order to survive on wild game. According to Dr. Eaton, this program is "the most successful ever launched for troubled youth." One year after their wilderness survival experience, only 15 percent of the participants have engaged in another crime. The program's field supervisor believes that taking animal's lives for food did the most to transform the boys by giving them "a sense of respect for life."

Hunting: A Vital Part of Rural North American Heritage

Unlike rodeo or fishing, hunting is a uniquely rural sport: even a tiny *.22-caliber* bullet can travel up to a mile and a half, so hunters must pursue their quarry in country and wilderness areas a safe distance away from settlements. Hunting also seems to form a sort of cultural divide between urban and rural residents. Many North American city dwellers despise or look down on hunting because it is far removed from their daily experience. Many rural families hunt and enjoy game meat, and for them, it is a normal part of life. Rural youth are much more likely than their urban counterparts to be sportsmen or sportswomen, as they have plenty of opportunities to hunt for recreation and to help provide food for their families.

A young hunter loads his rifle carefully. He knows that although hunting is a fun activity, it is also potentially dangerous.

For much of human history, hunting played a vital role in daily existence. Thirty thousand years ago, our Stone Age ancestors used spears, spear throwers, traps, ambushes, and other devices to fend off starvation and acquire necessary clothing and shelter. When Columbus blundered into the so-called New World, thousands of different *indigenous* cultures depended on hunting and fishing, as well as agriculture, for their survival. The European explorers, however, came from a different set of circumstances. Centuries before the "discovery" of the Americas, Europe's wild game was depleted, and ranchers and sheepherders replaced hunters as providers of meat for society. Wealthy landowners and nobles maintained private

Young hunters
need to carefully
observe all
safety rules.

forests stocked with deer, wild boar, pheasants, and other game for their own private hunting pleasure; commoners caught *poaching* on their lands were punished most severely.

As they conquered the Americas, Europeans quickly learned to take advantage of the abundant game available throughout the continent. In North America, frontier hunters such as Daniel Boone, Davy Crockett, and Buffalo Bill became legends. After finishing their conquest of Native peoples and establishing claim to the land, the settlers continued hunting until they had wiped out or endangered a number of species. For example, when Europeans arrived, seemingly infinite numbers of wild pigeons lived in the Americas, from Quebec in the north to Guatemala in the south, and from Pacific to Atlantic coasts. These pigeons were so abundant that at times flocks of them darkened the sky, and early settlers said they were "beyond number or imagination." These billions of wild pigeons were both a source of free food and a natural protection against pests that devoured crops and grains. To curtail the wild pigeon population, settlers went about shooting and trapping mass quantities of the seemingly inexhaustible flocks. They succeeded so well in harvesting the pigeons that by 1914, the American wild pigeon had become extinct. Of course, the pigeons were not unique as victims of over-hunting: bison, deer, elk, alligators, and other species were also hunted to the point of rarity or near-extinction.

In the early twentieth century, new forms of scientific wildlife management achieved an impressive reversal. While rarely discussed in popular literature, the accomplishments of wildlife *conservationists* in the United States during the 1900s were unprecedented and phenomenal. As odd as it may seem, sportsmen and sportswomen led the fight for wildlife restoration; they were first to set limits protecting game animals from extinction. Furthermore, sportsmen and sportswomen supported the new measures financially through hunting license fees, *excise taxes* on hunting and fishing equipment, and donations of time and energy to help develop habitats for wildlife.

By the late twentieth century, the efforts of wildlife biologists, hunters, and **anglers** achieved an astounding revitalization of wildlife in the United States. Today, deer wander into backyards and roadways even in urban areas like Detroit and the foothills of Los Angeles, and enormous elk saunter onto schoolyards in northern Arizona. Animals once near extinction now multiply in abundance.

Sadly, there are still more than fifty mammals and as many birds, reptiles, amphibians, and fish classified as endangered in North America. However, very few of these are games species, and hunting is not threatening them. The reason species now become endangered can often be traced to the loss of habitat due to expanding cities, chemical pollution, toxins, and climate change.

Declining Interest Among Teens Fosters Attempts to Revive Enthusiasm for Hunting

"If hunting were to die out, kids would lose their tie, their connection, to the land." That is the concern of Chris Moorman, an assistant forestry professor at North Carolina State University. He has reason to be concerned: teen interest in hunting seems to be waning. An article by Anne Blythe in the *Raleigh News & Observer* lists reasons for this decline. Many former hunting grounds have turned into suburban developments; fields and forests increasingly give way to housing and shopping malls. Urban teenagers must rely on adults to drive them miles from their homes to spend a day in the woods hunting. There are so many other things for teens to do with their time; computer games, after-school activities, and jobs crowd out outdoor recreation. Evidence of the increasing lack of interest in hunting is the decrease in the number of hunting licenses purchased

Wearing bright clothing is a safety measure that helps prevent hunters from accidentally shooting each other.

Hunting safety courses are a vital requirement for young adult hunters.

nationally; it has dropped to 14.7 million in 2003 from 16.4 million in 1983, according to the federal Fish and Wildlife Service.

States are using various means to lure young hunters back into the woods. A number of states now set aside special weekends or other very short seasons for adolescent hunters only. In Michigan, more than 20,000 twelve- to sixteen-year-olds will hit the woods on a September weekend to take part in the Michigan Department of Natural Resources' youth deer season. Only teens are allowed to hunt for those two days, though an adult must accompany them. Since Michigan began their special weekends in 2000, the number of hunters has grown by about one thousand teens each year, according to the state Department of Natural Resources. Hunting enthusiasts are encouraged that these numbers might indicate that the sport may see a comeback among youth in Michigan.

The state of Maine holds an annual Youth Deer Day hunt, and in 2004, 17,826 young hunters held a junior hunting license, and 599 tagged deer on Youth Deer Day. The number of junior hunting licenses sold has actually increased by several thousand over the past decade in that state, suggesting that such measures do encourage young sportsmen and sportswomen to get into the field.

Fourteen-year-old Donny was delighted with Youth Deer Day 2005. Accompanied by his father, Donny came upon a deer, sighted his gun on the deer's left shoulder, and fired. It was his first hunt, first shot, and first kill—a 151-pound six-point buck.

Training and Arms

Most states require that all individuals successfully complete hunter safety courses before receiving their licenses. Supervised by a state wildlife agency and staffed by qualified engineers, such courses usually require ten or more hours to complete. Subjects include firearm handling and safety, game identification, survival, first aid, and laws pertaining to hunting.

Two teenage hunters display a skin from an earlier hunt. For these young adults, hunting is an activity that fosters pride and a sense of achievement.

Dolly, seventeen, a native of Peña Blanca, New Mexico, was the only student in her gun-safety class to score a perfect 100 on the exam. As a result, she won a chance to hunt with a professional guide at Vermejo Park, a place that some sportsmen consider the most beautiful setting in northern New Mexico. Accompanied by her father and the guide, Dolly spotted a cow elk 200 yards (182.9 meters) away; she sighted her .308 rifle, steadied herself, pressed the trigger, and shot. "You hit it!" her dad said as the elk leaped away. Just as she had been taught in the hunter safety course, Dolly set out to track the elk's prints in the snow. She soon came upon the big animal's lifeless body; she had downed her first elk with one shot. She jumped up and down for joy, then gutted and cleaned the elk by her-

Steven was having trouble with his new muzzle-loading rifle; he couldn't get it to hit the same place consistently. This was especially frustrating because he is, literally, a rocket scientist who does research for NASA. Fortunately for Steven, his fourteen-year-old son Nicholas is a fellow member of the Double X Hunt Club in Surry, Virginia, and has a very inquiring mind. Nicholas examined all of the factors involved in the problem. Because his dad was using the same type of bullet and the same weight and type of powder, the eighth-grader decided the problem must lie with the percussion cap used to set off the charge. When Nicholas' father switched to a more expensive percussion cap, the gun started shooting accurately. Nicholas turned the problem and his solution into a science project that beat out two hundred other displays at his school's science fair.

self. Hunter safety training had really paid off for the young New Mexico hunter.

Depending on the type of game sought, hunters use a wide array of sporting arms. Small game requires a small-caliber rifle or shotgun; fowl requires a shotgun, and bigger game requires a larger-caliber rifle. Many hunters use compound bows to hunt during special bow seasons. Additionally, a number of states offer special seasons for muzzle-loading firearms. These are single-shot guns, loaded with a lead bullet and black powder from the front of the barrel. Muzzleloaders are the guns pioneers such as Daniel Boone, Davy Crockett, and Jeremiah Johnson would have used.

Hunting in the Twenty-First Century Can Be Controversial

Seventeen-year-old George took a shot with his .30-06 rifle and placed himself squarely in the middle of a raging controversy. It was November of 2005, and the opening day of a first-of-its kind hunt— the first legal hunt for Yellowstone National Park bison that wandered outside the park's boundary. As soon as George downed the bison, animal rights *activists* and reporters rushed in with cameras and questions. A reporter asked George how he felt about killing an animal with so much heritage. "Indifferent," said the young hunter. "It's really big." George's father suggested that activists were blowing the bison hunt out of proportion: "They're a big game animal that has been hunted for thousands of years. I'm not the first one to take part in [hunting them]." George's mother said many people were going to enjoy the meat.

More than ever in history, people in North America are concerned for the rights and happiness of animals—and that makes hunting controversial. Anti-hunting activists say that killing creatures for sport is cruel and unnecessary. Furthermore, they claim that hunters take a toll on endangered species and cause too many tragic accidents. On the other side, hunters claim they are among the foremost conservationists, helping maintain a necessary balance between species that works for all species' benefit, and that taxes paid by hunters have aided in the preservation of endangered species.

Hunting with a crossbow is another option some rural teens enjoy.

Hunting requires patience!

Safety Always
Comes First

A nine-year-old girl accidentally shot herself during the first day of Indiana's firearm deer season in November of 2005. According to officials, the girl slipped and fell while walking up a steep hill, causing her shotgun to fire, striking her in the shoulder. She was taken to a nearby hospital in critical condition.

Hunting can turn deadly when people are careless or irresponsible. In 1998, there were ninety-eight fatal hunting accidents, both in the United States and Canada. Most of these accidents would not have happened if hunters had followed the three basic rules for firearm safety listed in the sidebar.

Though hunting may be controversial, and it may be dangerous if people are irresponsible, thousands of teen sportsmen and sportswomen continue the sport. Take, for example, fifteen-year-old Lorianne from Marietta, Georgia. When she was still in diapers, Lorianne's parents brought her along to hunting camp. When she was ten, she learned to shoot a .22 rifle. When she was twelve, she killed her first deer. Lorianne has proven she can do everything the boys do, and then more. She wears mascara during deer hunts. Why? She told a reporter for *Georgia Outdoor News*, "You never know when a giant buck is going to come out, and I might have to pose for a picture."

CHAPTER 4
Fishing

Many Canadians recognize Rick Hansen because of his amazing Man in Motion World Tour, during which he crossed Canada and the globe in a wheelchair to raise money for spinal cord research. That tour raised $24 million, and his Rick Hansen Institute has since generated another $137 million for spinal cord research. While Hansen is famous as an inspiration for people with physical challenges, few people realize that the sport of fishing has influenced the *vicissitudes* of Rick's life. An article in *Outdoor Canada Online* by Jake MacDonald explains what angling has meant to Rick Hansen and how he is now trying to help one endangered marine species.

On a summer day in 1973, a group of teen boys was hitchhiking on the road that leads from Bella Coola, British Columbia, to Williams Lake. They had spent four exciting days camping in the Atnarko River Valley where they had caught big salmon and seen grizzly bear tracks. Rick had been fishing since he was three years old, and as a fifteen-year-old, he was happiest when enjoying the great outdoors.

A man driving a pickup truck pulled over to let the boys jump in the back, they piled in, and the truck took off down the rough road. Unfortunately, the boys did not realize the driver had been drinking alcohol. The truck veered into a ditch, throwing the boys and their fishing gear into the air. Rick hit the bottom of the ditch and felt an incredible pain in his back as his spine was broken.

For most of the next year, he was in a deep depression. He knew the rest of his life would be spent in a wheelchair, and he couldn't imagine being happy with such limitations. Then his father and his brother, Brad, persuaded Rick to get out of the house with them for a fishing trip. He recalls in the *Outdoor Canada* article,

> I guess I was ready to tuck it up and take a go at life. It turned out to be an incredible trip. . . . We drove up into the Thompson Valley, crossed a canyon on a swinging bridge with boards missing, went down a railway track, and climbed down this aggressive cliff with Brad carrying me on his back. We set up on a ledge by a boiling rapid and caught all these beautiful jack salmon. I couldn't believe the sensation of having those fish on the line. It made me realize that my life wasn't over at all.

Recently, Rick Hansen has taken up a new cause—helping the endangered Fraser River sturgeon to survive. In 1997, anglers encountered big sturgeon floating dead in the Fraser River, and Rick and others feared the fish were in trouble. He says, "We knew that concern was shared by many others. So my friends and I just decided we would start a society for conserving the sturgeon." The sturgeon are very ancient fish; their ancestors swam in rivers alongside the

Fishing is a pastime that has enriched the lives of many rural young people.

Many children growing up in the country learn about relationships and working together while on a fishing trip.

dinosaurs, and these prehistoric survivors are suitably gigantic, weighing up to 1,000 pounds and reaching over twelve feet long. Fraser and members of his organization catch and tag the giant fish. The fish are then released, and their movements tracked.

Rick credits his healthy outlook on life and his impressive achievements to the lessons his father and brother taught him while fishing, "It really changed my way of thinking," he says.

I always thought you had to be able to go it alone to be a man. But going fishing with my friends and family, helping them however I could, and letting them help me, taught me that you can't be a real man until you learn to be interdependent. You have to be part of a web of people. Whether you're talking about a family or a community or a society, you have to learn to work with others toward common goals.

Fishing Is a Universal Sport

Norman Maclean begins his novel *A River Runs Through It* by saying, "In our family, there was no clear line between religion and fly fishing." While some anglers might not use the word "religion," most agree that the art of fishing puts them in touch with a reality greater than themselves—participation in the great wilderness and the courting of good fortune. Fishing comes to mean more than just pursuit of the scaly slippery creature. It includes the companionship of family and friends, long hours together on the water, and relaxed evenings telling stories about "the big one that got away." Like other outdoor sports, fishing helps rural teens stay connected with traditions that go back far before their time.

People were fishing before they began recording history. In almost every human culture around the world, fish provided a vital source of healthy nutrition. From frozen arctic wastes to steaming jungles, from tiny desert streams to vast pounding oceans, men and women survived by using a variety of techniques to haul in their catches. In the twenty-first century, some people continue to fish for survival, but it is less common today than in past times. Fish farms provide much of the aquatic fare that finds its way to our dinner plates, and depleted stock of ocean fish are increasingly finding protection under federal laws. At the same time, the sport of fishing is undiminished.

Today, an adult may take some girl or boy on his or her first fishing trip. For instance, she may walk to the end of the Seal Beach Pier in southern California, or sit in the *prow* of a boat motoring down the Susquehanna River in Upstate New York, or hike through the forest to a remote lake in the Alberta wilderness. He may carry an elegant fly rod for casting in a freshwater stream, or a long strong surf rod for fishing off the ocean beach, or maybe simply an inexpensive rod and line purchased the night before from Wal-Mart. Wherever, how ever, they are equipped to join the vast ranks of sport anglers. In the United States, 34 million people fish for fun and recreation, and there were 3.6 million active adult anglers in Canada in 2000. In 2000, U.S. anglers paid $491 million dollars for fishing licenses, tags, permits, and stamps issued by the Fish and Wildlife Service.

Teens and children are among the most avid anglers throughout North America. Young people have excellent hand-eye coordination and are as capable of prize catches as any adult. As any angler will tell you, the sport isn't just about skill; sheer luck plays an important role in determining success, and an eight-year-old can get just as lucky as a forty-year-old. For these reasons, teens are enthusiastic participants in the sport.

Sport fishing is by no means limited to rural enthusiasts; there are anglers fishing the streams and lakes of vast urban centers. However, rural youth do enjoy certain benefits over their city counterparts when it comes to fishing. As Celeste Carmichael notes in the introduction to this series, "Rural youth spend more time than

Fishing memories are made in many places—on piers, in little rowboats, and on ocean beaches.

their urban counterparts in contact with . . . nature . . . and they benefit from . . . their understanding of the natural world." Rural anglers enjoy fishing in *tranquil* streams, forest-lined lakes, or lonely stretches of seaside. Furthermore, there are fishing opportunities not far from most rural areas.

Fly Fishing

One of the most sophisticated forms of angling is fly fishing, a sport common to rural ponds and rivers. Fly fishing works best in areas where water runs quickly over a gravel bottom, then deepens slightly and runs more slowly. Trout like to bask in such areas where the water is clean and well **oxygenated**. Fly fishers must wade in the water, wearing rubber waders (boots extending up to the waist) to do so. Fly rods are specially made; they must be lightweight, with just the right flex and balance so an angler can cast and hold the rod all day without becoming sore or fatigued. Fly-casting is a fine art in itself, beginning with a back cast (the line goes behind the angler) then whistling forward as the rod flexes the opposite way. This is tricky to learn, but expert fly fishers can put their hooks right where they want them.

The goal of fly fishing is to imitate a living insect by using an artificial one. Anglers who do this develop a deep knowledge of fish, their feeding habits, and insects and their behaviors. As the fish closes in on the fly, the angler must wield his rod and fly in an intricate dance that convinces the fish this is genuine prey. There are literally thousands of different flies used for this sport, and preparation of an angler's fly is itself an art. Many fly fishers make their own lures using feathers, thread, and various artificial components.

Sixteen-year-old Jeff, who lives in southwestern Michigan, has the perfect job for a teenager—he gets to work in his own home, listen to his favorite music, be his own boss, and still make money. He

A "fly" is designed to trick fish into thinking it is an insect.

It's important that young fishers learn safety precautions.

began fly fishing with his father at the age of ten, and now manufactures and sells flies. Fly fishing is not only an art, it also involves total consistency: if a customer orders 100 lures of a certain type, Jeff needs to make sure that each one is the same size, shape, color, and weight. Despite the difficult nature of his work, he wouldn't trade his job for anything else.

Safety

An article posted on Outdoor Central Web site reports,

> A weary sadness is audible in Water Patrol Sgt. Paul Kennedy's voice when he tells the story of Missouri's most recent hunting-related boating fatality. Sadness because the victim was only 14 years old. The weariness comes from seeing similar circumstances involved in so many boating deaths. . . . "It's no different than what is occurring all over the nation," said Kennedy, who is director of public information and safety education for the Water Patrol. "Time and again, hunters and anglers fail to take simple precautions that could save their lives."

One out of three U.S. citizens who die each year while boating are hunters or anglers. While fishing is fun, it can also be dangerous if anglers do not take common-sense precautions. For starters, always wear a life preserver on a boat, and have throwable flotation devices handy as well. Nine out of ten fatal boating accidents involve people who are not wearing their life jackets. Boaters should also carry a noise-making device such as a whistle or horn, a flare gun, and a first-aid kit with them at all times. They should avoid standing up when the boat is in motion, and make sure that all equipment and catches are safely stowed so they won't slide around in the boat.

An increasing problem in pleasure boating and fishing from a boat is drunken fishing. Never, ever go fishing in a boat with someone who has had too much to drink. And if someone is drinking while in the boat, make sure there is someone along to be the designated "driver" or rower.

Even if an angler is not in a boat, fishing may still prove hazardous. Wading in any river can be dangerous. Even for an experienced angler, unavoidable hazards may lurk in swift or deep water. Fly fishers can drown when water gets into their waders, causing the angler to be swept away by the river current, or they may suffer from *hypothermia*, so anglers must never go in water deeper than their waders. They should also make sure their rubber boots are in good shape with no leaks.

Anglers also need to remember that a fishhook can be a dangerous thing—and not just to the fish. Always handle the hook by its shank, otherwise you risk getting the point of the hook stuck in your hand. Store hooks in a small piece of cork or foam, so you will not pierce yourself grabbing hooks from the tackle box. Be very aware of where other people are when casting; if you have never fished before, you might want to have someone else cast for you; nasty accidents can occur when anglers hook nearby people when attempting to cast.

Environmental Issues

Teenagers living in a rural area may not be concerned about ecology issues in connection with fishing. After all, the land still looks pretty much the way it did when her grandparents were alive, and there are still plenty of fish in the local pond, so why be concerned? However, even for rural youth, there are ecological issues to think about. Global climate change influences the amount of water in lakes and streams, and pollutants in the atmosphere are affecting the plants, insects, and small forms of animal life that fish depend on to live. Furthermore, chemicals getting into the water and lead from hunters' shot can settle on the bottom of lakes, affecting fish and

Environmental issues are important to fishers, whether they realize it or not. Water pollution can destroy fish populations or make them unsafe to eat.

Fishing has played a role in American rural culture for several hundred years.

Commercial fishers compete with recreational anglers for diminished fish populations.

making them unhealthy to eat. So even in remote and beautiful areas, anglers need to be concerned about the health of the fish, and the health of the angler eating them.

Controversy exists today between recreational anglers (who fish for sport) and commercial fishers (who catch fish in order to sell them), caused largely by declining numbers of fish, both in freshwater and ocean environments. Overfishing by recreational and commercial fishers has caused shortages of fish species, especially in saltwater. Government restrictions have been placed on some areas of fishing, and it is these restrictions that are causing conflict between the two groups of people who love fishing. Those who fish for recreation tend to blame the commercial ocean harvesters for shortages of fish, and conversely, those who make their living from the ocean feel they have a right to take every kind of fish that recreational anglers go after.

Because of the declining number of fish in the world's oceans, an increasing proportion of fish sold in markets are raised in fish farms; the raising of fish in tanks for commercial purposes is called aquaculture. Aquaculture allows wild fish stock to replenish and increase in their natural environments. Catfish, striped bass, salmon, and trout are especially common stock in fish farms.

Competitive fishing tournaments are also controversial. These tournaments offer substantial prizes for entrants who catch the biggest fish, such as large mouth bass. In these events, a professional angler and an amateur angler usually fish from the same boat. Since the goal is to catch the biggest fish, and since the parties on different boats have no way to know if they have the biggest fish until they get back to the dock, they tend to kill most of the big fish they catch; hence critics charge that such tournaments cause unnecessary killing. Critics argue that even tournaments that are strictly "catch and release" still wind up killing hundreds of bass that are injured by fishing hooks and the shock of being caught; furthermore, these dying fish are thrown back and wasted—is that any more humane than catching and killing a fish that will be eaten and not wasted? Competition anglers and anglers who fish to supplement their families' food supply blame one another for overfishing.

The debate over tournaments ties into a larger debate: catch and release versus catch and kill fishing. If you catch and release, you must be careful how you do so. Wet your hands before handling a fish in order not to damage the coating of mucus that enables a fish to swim quickly and to avoid disease. Only keep it out of the water for a very brief time; a fish out of water is in distress. Stay calm and don't panic, even if a fish thrashes or sticks your hand with its fins. Release the fish under the water, holding it for a few moments first so it can re-adapt to its climate before release.

Birds and other animals also compete with human beings for fish.

Like many country children, this boy is learning young the pleasures of fishing.

Confessions of a Teenage Angler

"In my family, we all love fishing, and we begin learning from the time we get out of diapers." That's what sixteen-year-old Sarah says in an article published on the GORP Web site. Sarah began fishing with what she now calls "a little Mickey Mouse outfit" and used worms for bait. She only managed to catch little brook trout, "but we thought each one was Moby Dick." When Sarah was seven, she got her first fly rod and reel as a present. She says, "The coolest thing is that I actually caught a fish on one of my first casts, using only a fly, and landed it myself." Sarah knows that not all teens enjoy fishing, but she wishes they could share the benefits she has gained from the sport. She says, "they can be in the wilderness, discovering things that they would never see anywhere else. I would never have seen a huge waterfall with a rainbow behind it, big bear footprints, or deer running across a stream without fishing. I also wouldn't have all these great memories of spending time with my family. There are things that you just can't get anywhere else but out on some stream, and I am appreciative to my family for sharing the sport of fishing with me. So get off the couch, turn off the TV, and go hook a fish!"

Gar are really
weird-looking!

A Really Weird Fish—But It Led Him to a Prize

Gars are a member of the pike family, and they are among the nastiest looking denizens of freshwaters. They've been around since Jurassic times, and they look as mean as their prehistoric ancestors. Gar are covered with bony scales, a feature that makes them tough to kill and even tougher to prepare for eating. They are edible, but most anglers do not care for the taste. However, none of these facts bothers Zach, a fifteen-year-old sophomore at Minooka High School in Illinois, who loves to fish for gar in the Vermillion River. Gar are tricky to catch, and thus present anglers with an entertaining challenge.

In July of 2005, Zach and his brother were fishing for gar when Zach inadvertently snagged something bigger—a huge fifty-five pound flathead catfish that was forty inches long and had a twenty-five-inch girth. What did he do then? Zach says, "My brother took about twenty-six photos of me with the fish. After we weighed and measured it, we just let it go. Maybe some day I'll catch it again or someone else will be able to catch it." Although he released the fish, Zach's achievement did not go unnoticed: he qualified for induction into the National Fresh Water Fishing Hall of Fame for a World Record Catch and Release Angling Achievement.

This young man caught and released a smallmouth bass in the Boundary Canoe Waters Area in Minnesota near the U.S.–Canada border.

National Teen Anglers

Teen Anglers is a nonprofit organization committed to teaching young people boating and fishing skills. They seek to "provide an opportunity for all teens to participate in a no-fee program that will teach them the art of fishing, conservation, and essential details of boating with emphasis on safety." According to the organization's Web site, educating young people about fishing enables them to gain knowledge in many other areas, including "Outdoors Photography, Biology, Ecology, Meteorology, Astronomy, Geography, Chemistry, Topography and all the Physical Sciences." Furthermore, Teen Anglers aims to keep youthful sports enthusiasts off drugs and alcohol.

Anglers also need to be respectful of other people and other creatures that share the rural environment with them. If you are out in the wild, be courteous and thoughtful of those around you. Kingfishers, otters, beaver, deer, and other animals share the lakes and ponds where you fish and deserve to go about their business without being disturbed. Always pick up your soda cans or bottles, candy wrappers, and other debris. Remember that something as small as the ring around a water bottle top can become deadly if

Fishing is a vital part of North America's cultural heritage.

swallowed by wildlife. Never trespass; always obey signs posted on people's property. Don't crank loud music out of your radio in the wilderness where people go to relax and enjoy the sounds of nature. (Besides, it will scare the fish.) Take notice of waterside signs; these include notices on how many fish anglers can take and warnings about **wake** restrictions or dangers in the water.

Angling is a sport that millions of Canadians and U.S. citizens continue to enjoy each year, and it is a vital part of North America's outdoor heritage. At the same time, today's teen anglers must be increasingly aware that their recreation affects other people, both anglers and nonanglers. Today's rural youth share an obligation to their neighbors and to future generations to protect and cherish water life, other wildlife, and the natural environment.

Further Reading

Bailey, John. *The Young Fishing Enthusiast: A Practical Guide for Kids*. New York: DK, 1999.

Budd, Jackie. *The Complete Guide to Horses and Ponies: Understanding Horses and Ponies*. Milwaukee, Wis.: Gareth Stevens Publishing, 1999.

Elman, Robert. *Hunting Allies*. Broomall, Pa.: Mason Crest, 2002.

Elman, Robert. *Hunting Arms*. Broomall, Pa.: Mason Crest, 2002.

Elman, Robert. *Nature*. Broomall, Pa.: Mason Crest, 2002.

Hansen, Jens Plough. *Spinning & Baitcasting*. Broomall, Pa.: Mason Crest, 2003.

Jeffrey, Laura S. *American Humane Pet Care Library: Horses: How to Choose and Care for a Horse*. Berkley Heights, N.J.: Enslow, 2004.

Johannesson, Per Ola. *Baitfishing*. Broomall, Pa.: Mason Crest, 2003.

Nordin, Hans. *Ice Fishing*. Broomall, Pa.: Mason Crest, 2003.

Oglesby, A., Kreh, L., Ulnitz, S. *Flyfishing*. Broomall, Pa.: Mason Crest, 2003.

Olsson, Jan. *Trolling*. Broomall, Pa.: Mason Crest, 2003.

Sherman, Josepha. *Rodeo Bull Riding*. Chicago, Ill.: Heinemann Library, 2000.

Solomon, Dane. *Fishing: Have Fun, Be Smart*. New York: Rosen, 2000.

Walberg, Anders. *The Sport Fisherman's Cookbook*. Broomall, Pa.: Mason Crest, 2003.

Weaver, Jack. *Hunting: Have Fun, Be Smart*. New York: Rosen, 2000.

Wessman, Bo. *Building Your Own Rod*. Broomall, Pa.: Mason Crest, 2003.

For More Information

American Junior Rodeo Association
mysite.verizon.net/resp1qhq

Committee to Abolish Sport Hunting
www.all-creatures.org/cash/home.html

Flyfishingconnection.com
www.flyfishingconnection.com/

GORP.com your encyclopedic resource for outdoor recreation
gorp.away.com/index.html

Hunt of a Lifetime: Making Dreams Come True
www.huntofalifetime.org/index.shtml

Jessica Jahiel's Horse Sense
www.horse-sense.org

National Rifle Association Hunting Facts
www.nraila.org/Issues/FactSheets/Read.aspx?ID=124

National Teen Anglers
www.teenanglers.org

Outdoors Magazine
www.vermontoutdoors.com/index.asp

Teen Sportsment Online
www.geocities.com/juniorhunters

Publisher's note:
The Web sites listed on this page were active at the time of publication. The publisher is not responsible for Web sites that have changed their addresses or discontinued operation since the date of publication. The publisher will review and update the Web-site list upon each reprint.

Glossary

activists: People who work to create positive change in the world.

anglers: People who fish with a hook, line, and rod.

bit: The part of the bridle that fits in a horse's mouth.

blind: A hiding place from which hunters shoot their prey.

bond: The act of linking that binds individuals together in a relationship.

caliber: The diameter of a bullet or shell.

conservationists: People who work to protect natural resources.

equestrians: Relating to horseback riding.

excise taxes: Additional money that consumers pay on certain goods' prices.

gait: The pattern of a horse's steps.

genetics: The scientific study of heredity.

hippology: The study of horses.

hypothermia: Abnormally low body temperature.

indigenous: Native to an area.

Mad Cow Disease: A disease that affects the nervous system of cows.

muck: To clean out.

oxygenated: Supplied with oxygen.

peers: Individuals who share characteristics, such as age, income, or background.

poaching: Taking something from someone else's property without permission.

prow: Front of a ship.

rack: Antlers, usually referring to a deer, elk, or moose.

tranquil: Quiet, peaceful.

vicissitudes: Unexpected changes.

vocationally: Having to do with the pursuit of a job or occupation.

wake: The path left by a moving body (such as a boat) in a fluid (such as water).

Bibliography

Bailey, John. *The Young Fishing Enthusiast: A Practical Guide for Kids.* New York: DK, 1999.

Budd, Jackie. *The Complete Guide to Horses and Ponies: Horse and Pony Care.* Milwaukee: Gareth Stevens Publishing, 1998.

Budd, Jackie. *The Complete Guide to Horses and Ponies: Understanding Horses and Ponies.* Milwaukee, Wis.: Gareth Stevens Publishing, 1999.

Canada.com. "Rodeo Kids Buck Farm Adversity." http://www.canada.com/edmonton/edmontonjournal/news/story.html?id= 83c01afa-e331-46f0-97d3-0d5fccba7cfc.

ChannelOne.com. "Why I Hunt." http://channelone.com/news/exchange/opinions/2003/11/06/se_hunt.

Committee to Abolish Sport Hunting: Hunting Accident File. http://www.all-creatures.org/cash/taah-sh-20051112-2.html.

Conservation Force. "Why Hunting is Good Medicine for Society, Youth and the Environment." http://www.conservationforce.org/wwh/get_articles.cfm?id=31.

Courier-Journal.com. "Teen Angler Catches Dream Trip to Florida." http://www.courierJournal.com/apps/pbcs.dll/article?AID=/ 20051113/SPORTS/511130608/1002/SPORTS.

Detroit News. "Young Michigan Hunters get the Woods to Themselves." http://www.detnews.com/2005/outdoors/0511/12/B01-324612.htm.

Extinction of the American Passenger Pigeon. http://www.wildbirds.org/apidesay.htm.

Float Tube and Kayak Fishing Network. "Catch & Release vs Catch & Kill." http://www.fkpfishing.net/Articles/articles.C&R_vs_C&K.htm.

Foothills Lighthorse 4H Club. http://www.glcn.com/town/clubs/4-h/4-h.htm.

Free New Mexican. "Young Blood."
http://www.freenewmexican.com/news/8040.html.

Free Republic. "Two Teens ride Horses to School."
http://www.freerepublic.com/focus/f-news/1491454/post.

Georgia Outdoor News. "Cobb County Teen is Queen of the Woods."
http://www.gon.com/Lorianne905.html.

HelenaIR.com. First Bison taken by Belgrade Teen.
http://www.helenair.com/articles/2005/11/16/montana_top/a01111605_
01.txt.

History of 4H.
http://www.ext.nodak.edu/4h/history.htm.

Hook & Bait. "Statistics on Hunting and Fishing."
http://www.findarticles.com/p/articles/mi_m4021/is_2002_Nov_1/ai_
93089455.

Hunt of a Lifetime. "One Last Shot."
http://www.huntofalifetime.org/cgi-bin/news/news.pl?record=9.

Indystar.com. "Hunters Strive to Ssave a Dying Sport."
http://www.indystar.com/apps/pbcs.dll/article?AID=/20051016/
LIVING/510160363/1007/LIVING.

Jefferson County 4-H Program.
http://ces.ca.uky.edu/jefferson/youthdev/horse.htm.

Jessica Jahiel's Horse Sense.
http://www.horse-sense.org/stories/20050301181229.phtml.

Lincoln Way Sun. "Teen Makes Record Catch."
http://www.suburbanchicagonews.com/sunpub/lway/sports/j02lwout.htm.

MacDonald, Jake. "The Secret of His Success."
http://www.outdoorcanada.ca/fish/secret_his_success.shtml.

Mainetoday.com. "Outdoors: A Fast First For Youth Day Deer Hunter."
.http://outdoors.mainetoday.com/news/051023youthdeer.shtml.

NASD. "Injuries from Horses and Cows."
http://www.cdc.gov/nasd/docs/d000401-d000500/d000418/d000418.html.

National Agriculture Library. "Elsie Carper Collection on Extension
Service, Home Economics, and 4-H Biographical Sketch."
http://www.nal.usda.gov/speccoll/findaids/carper/biogrph.htm.

Navajo Times. "Family Tradition."
http://un-equaled.com/NTBLOG/?p=383 (November 23, 2005).

Outdoor Central. "Hunters, Anglers at High Risk for Boating Deaths."
http://www.outdoorcentral.com/mc/pr/04/02/13C1.asp.

Patent, Dorothy Hinshaw. *A Family Goes Hunting*. New York: Houghton Mifflin, 1991.

Poplar Bluff, *Daily American Republic*. "Danny lived his life on the back of a Bull."
http://www.darnews.com/articles/2003/08/25/news/news19.txt.

"Riden' for your life."
http://www.nod-valley.k12.ia.us/students/2003/lbthebest/index.html.

Rural Injuries PDF.
http://www.preventinjury.org/PDFs/RURAL_INJURY.pdf.

Sherman, Josepha. *Rodeo Bull Riding*. Chicago: Heinemann Library, 2000.

Solomon, Dane. *Fishing: Have Fun, Be Smart*. New York: Rosen, 2000.

"Teen Angler Ties Flies for Profit."
http://www.detnews.com/2001/metro/0103/28/c07w-204982.htm.

Teen Anglers Homepage.
www.teenanglers.org.

Tennessee Walking Horse Youth Association: 4-H Program.
http://www.twhbea.com/youth/4h.htm.

University of Tennessee. 4-H Horse Program.
http://animalscience.ag.utk.edu/horses/horse_bowl_hippology_results2005.htm.

The Virginian Pilot. "Teen's Determination Solves Dad's Dilemma."
http://scholar.lib.vt.edu/VA-news/VAPilot/issues/1996/vp960131/01300150.htm.

Williams, Sara Denise. "Teaching Kids to Fish: A Teenage Fisher Tells All."
http://gorp.away.com/gorp/activity/fishing/features/teaching_kids4.htm.

Zeaman, John. *Climbing onto the Horse's Back*. New York: Franklin Watts, 1998.

Index

Picture Credits

Harding House Publishing Service, Ben Stewart: pp. 25, 27, 43, 45, 46, 49, 50, 53, 54, 56, 60
iStockphotos:
   DeLillo, Jim: p. 82
   DeNijs, Michel: p.59
   Jakobsson, Jon: p. 86
   Peters, George: p. 84
   Ross, Angie: p. 80
Jupiter Images: pp. 28, 30, 33, 37, 38, 41, 62, 65, 66, 69, 71, 72, 75, 76, 77, 79
Libal, Steve: p. 22
McIntosh, Kenneth: pp. 8, 10, 11, 13, 16, 19, 21

To the best knowledge of the publisher, all other images are in the public domain. If any image has been inadvertently uncredited, please notify Harding House Publishing Service, Vestal, New York 13850, so that rectification can be made for future printings.

Biographies

Author

Roger Smith worked for over a decade as a junior high school teacher, and is currently a freelance writer. He enjoys living in beautiful northern Arizona, amid one of the world's largest ponderosa pine forests. His proudest sporting achievement is spearing a gar by means of a primitive atlatl and dart. Contrary to common opinion, he thinks gar are rather tasty.

Series Consultant

Celeste J. Carmichael is a 4-H Youth Development Program Specialist at the Cornell University Cooperative Extension Administrative Unit in Ithaca, New York. She provides leadership to statewide 4-H Youth Development efforts including communications, curriculum, and conferences. She communicates the needs and impacts of the 4-H program to staff and decision makers, distributing information about issues related to youth and development, such as trends for rural youth.